invasive

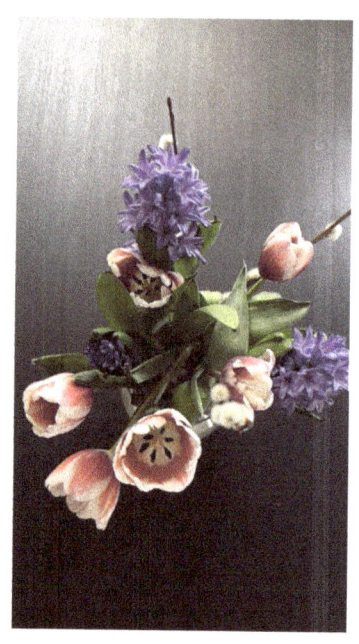

Jùmọ̀kẹ́ Gíwá

Invasive

Published by Fikún Inc.

Copyright © 2023 by Jùmọ̀kẹ́ Gíwá

jumokegiwa.com

Invasive #2 Well & Wealthy

All rights reserved, including the right of reproduction in whole or in part in any form.

Summary: Reflecting on spaces, places, and materials that are useful for nurturing and protecting wellness and wealth. Today is the tomorrow we talked about yesterday.

Dedication

For the vulnerable.

Breathe

Chapters

1. different view — 1
2. interactions — 5
3. serene space — 9
4. essential — 13
5. siloed — 17
6. pathologize — 21
7. thinking — 25
8. suddenly — 29
9. displaced — 33
10. purposeful — 37
11. read & write — 41
12. grounded — 45
13. foot soldier — 49
14. heart — 53
15. gaslighting on steroids — 57
16. faulty activism — 61
17. acknowledge. address. accommodate. — 65
18. pregnant silence — 69
19. gratitude attitude — 73
20. got it! — 77
21. rituals — 81
22. east looking west — 85

Breathe

breathe

different view

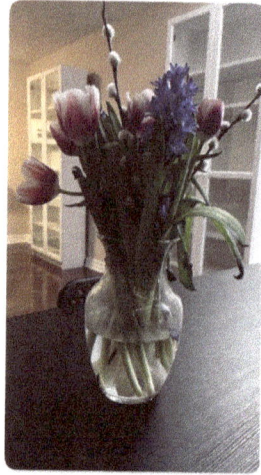
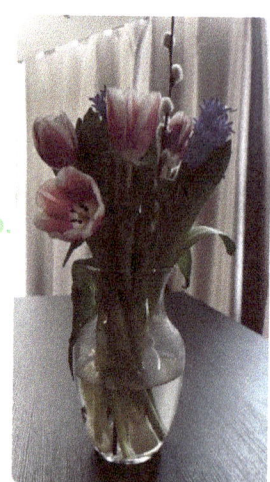

Enhance.
Accentuate.
Effect change.
Disrupt the status quo.

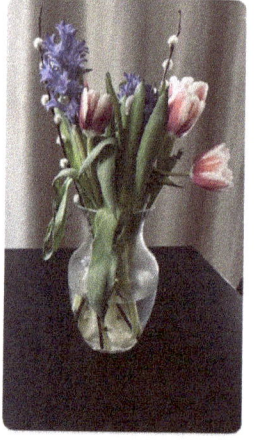

different view

Enhance.
Accentuate.
Effect change.
Disrupt the status quo.

Breathe

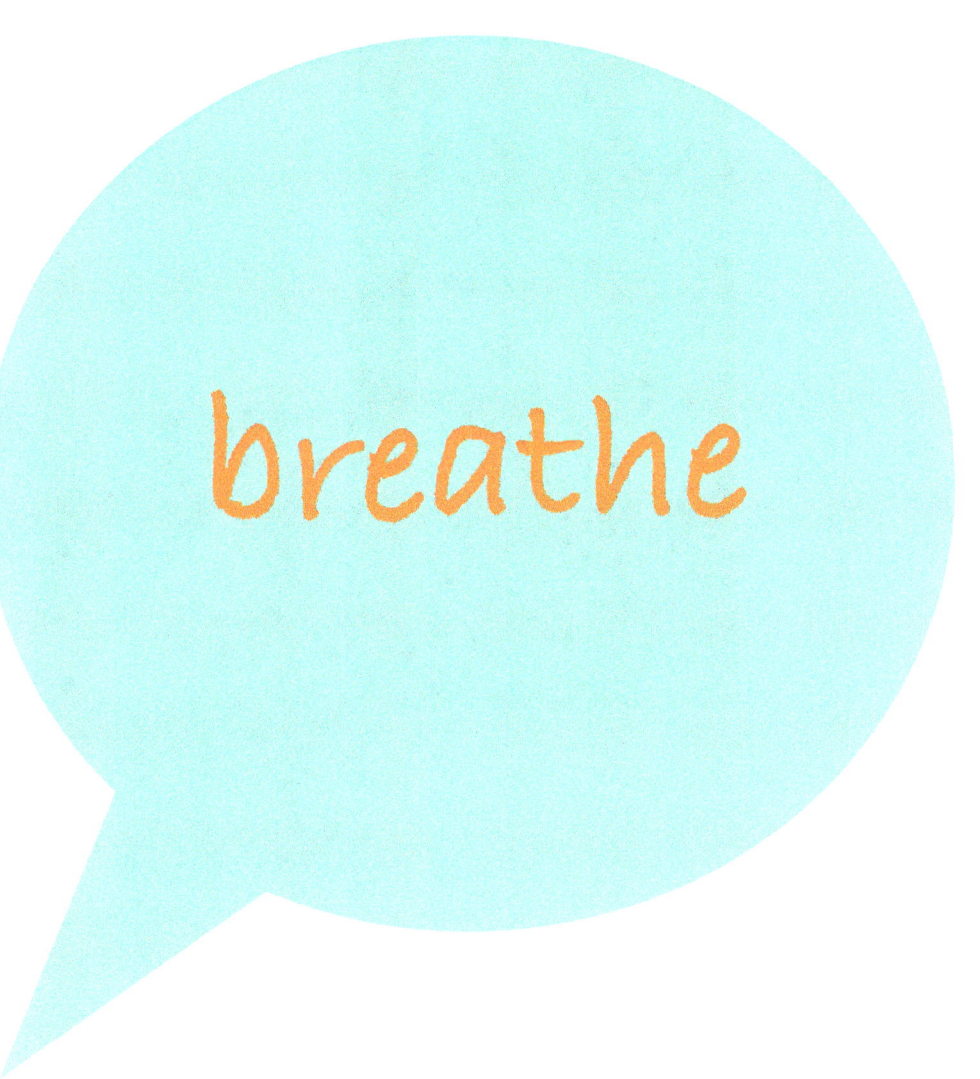

interactions

fulfilling & purposeful
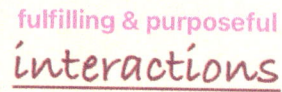

Emotions run high and low.
Thoughts travel far and wide.
Gut-wrenching feelings of helplessness
are interrupted by and interlaced with
brief moments of hopefulness.
Today is not a good day.
Today is a good day.
Every day is a good day.

interactions

Fulfilling and purposeful interactions.
Emotions run high and low.
Thoughts travel far and wide.
Gut-wrenching feelings of helplessness
are interrupted by and interlaced with
brief moments of hopefulness.

Today is not a good day.
Today is a good day.
Every day is a good day.

Breathe

breathe

serene space

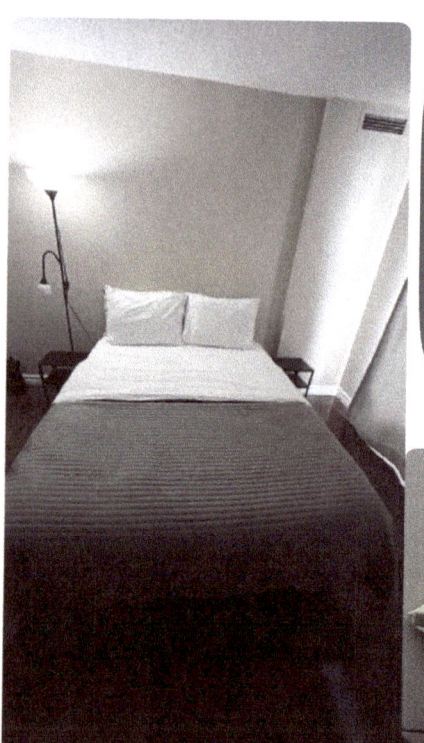

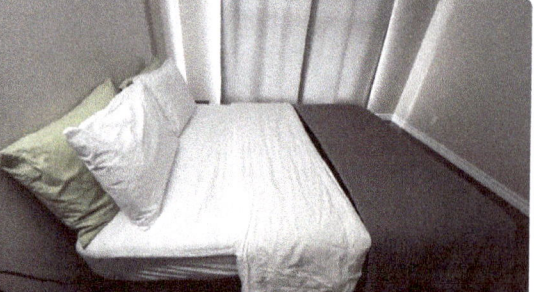

Loss. Grief. Displacement.
Isolated. Dismayed. Delayed.
Fog. Hibernation. Separation.
Chilling pause. Walk through. Drive over.
In the eagerness to turn the next page,
reaped the previous one off the book.

Slow down. Keep pace.
Read. Write. Reflect.
Joy. Peace. Hope.
Mindful. Grateful. Thoughtful.
In the serenity of this quiet space,
finding ways to move towards the good.

serene space

Loss. Grief. Displacement.
Isolated. Dismayed. Delayed.
Fog. Hibernation. Separation.
Chilling pause. Walk through. Drive over.
In the eagerness to turn the next page,
reaped the previous one off the book.

Slow down. Keep pace.
Read. Write. Reflect.
Joy. Peace. Hope.
Mindful. Grateful. Thoughtful.
In the serenity of this quiet space,
finding ways to move towards the good.

Breathe

breathe

essential

Essential yet berated, undervalued, overlooked, diminished.
Flow, water, flow. I don't take you for granted. I appreciate you.
Clean, water, clean. Head. Face. Mouth. Hands. Feet.
Run, water, run. Refreshing. Calming. Warming. Cooling.

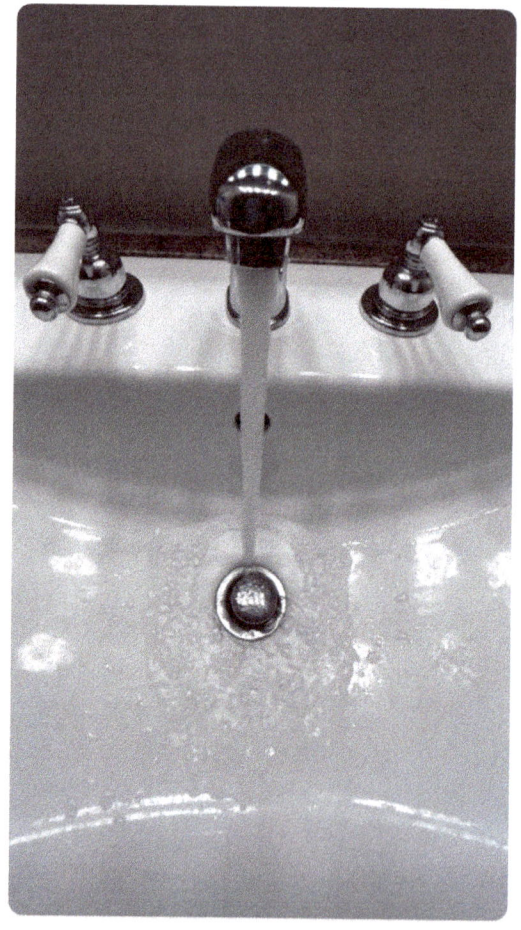

<u>essential</u>

Essential yet berated, undervalued, overlooked, diminished.

Flow, water, flow.
I don't take you for granted.

I appreciate you.

Clean, water, clean.
Head. Face. Mouth. Hands. Feet.

Run, water, run.
Refreshing. Calming. Warming. Cooling.

Breathe

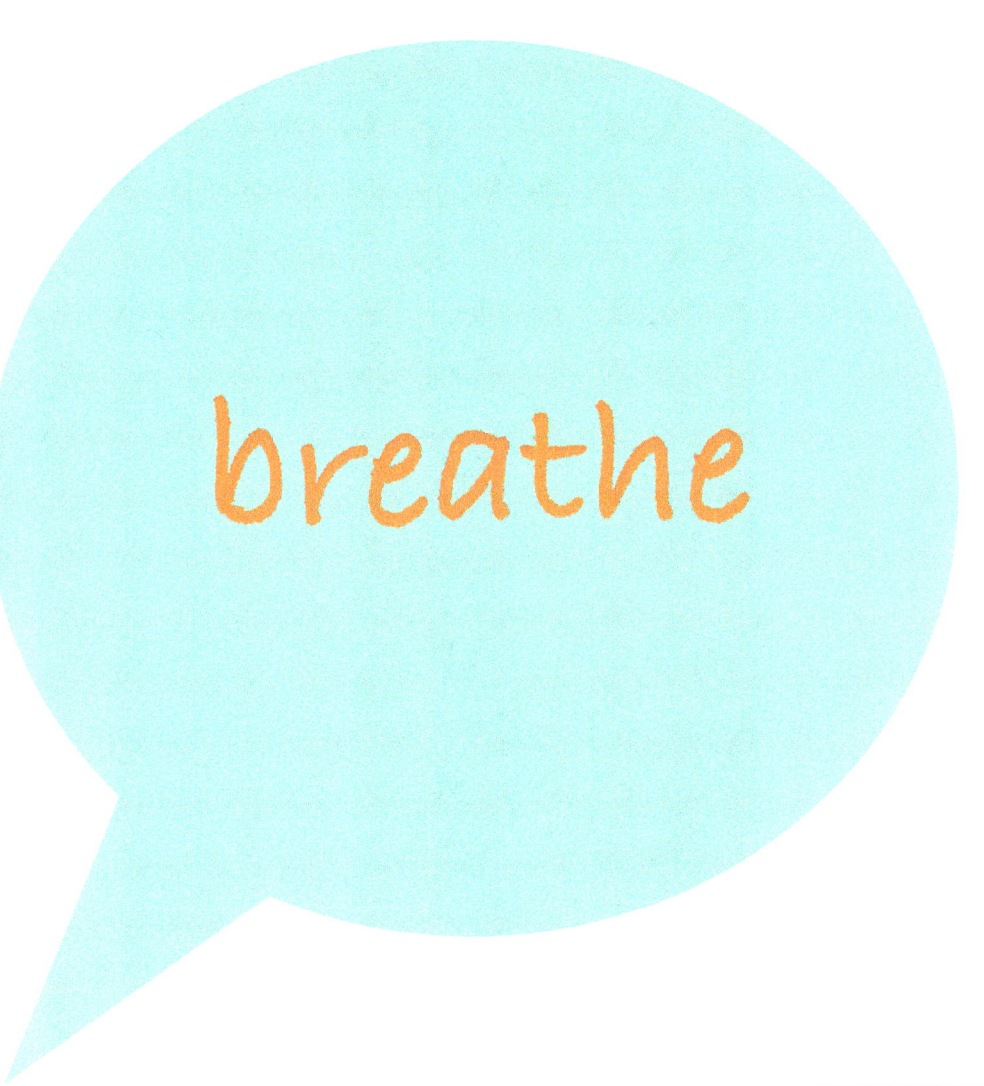

siloed

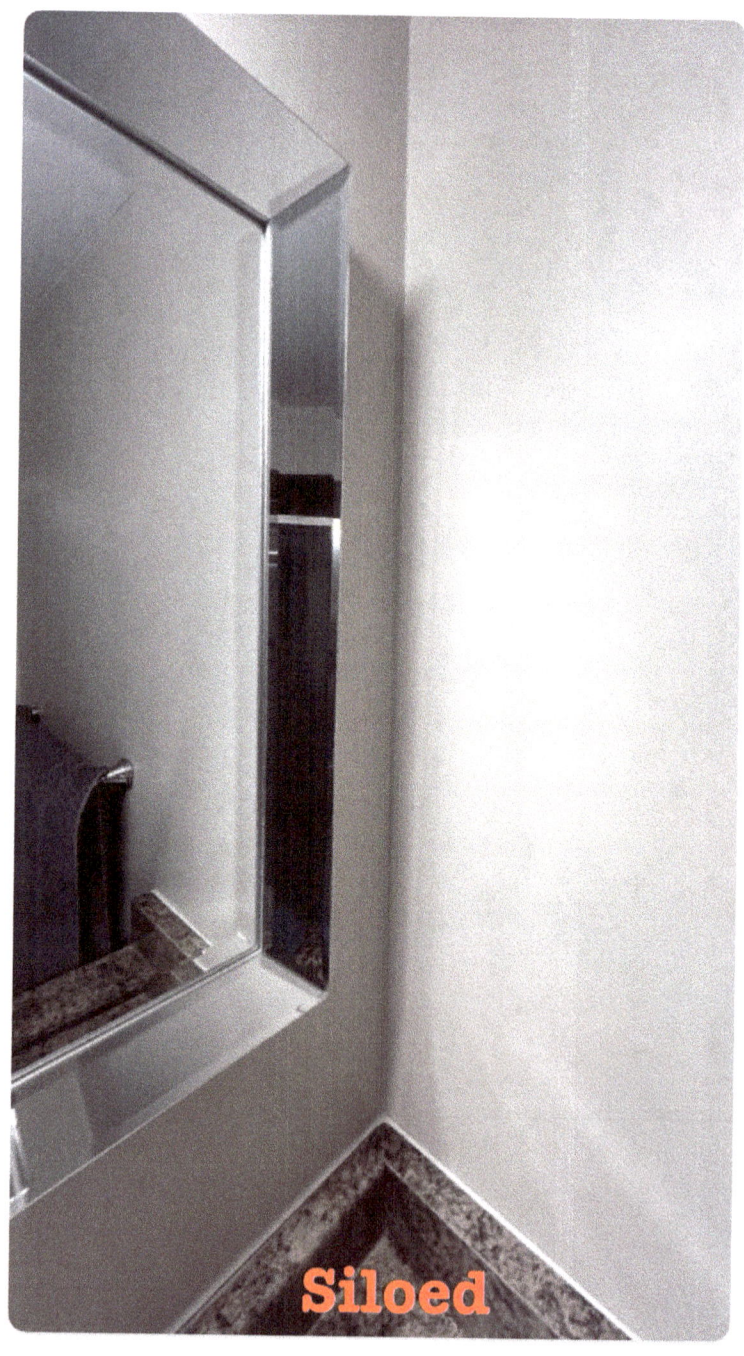

siloed

Siloed.

Breathe

breathe

pathologize

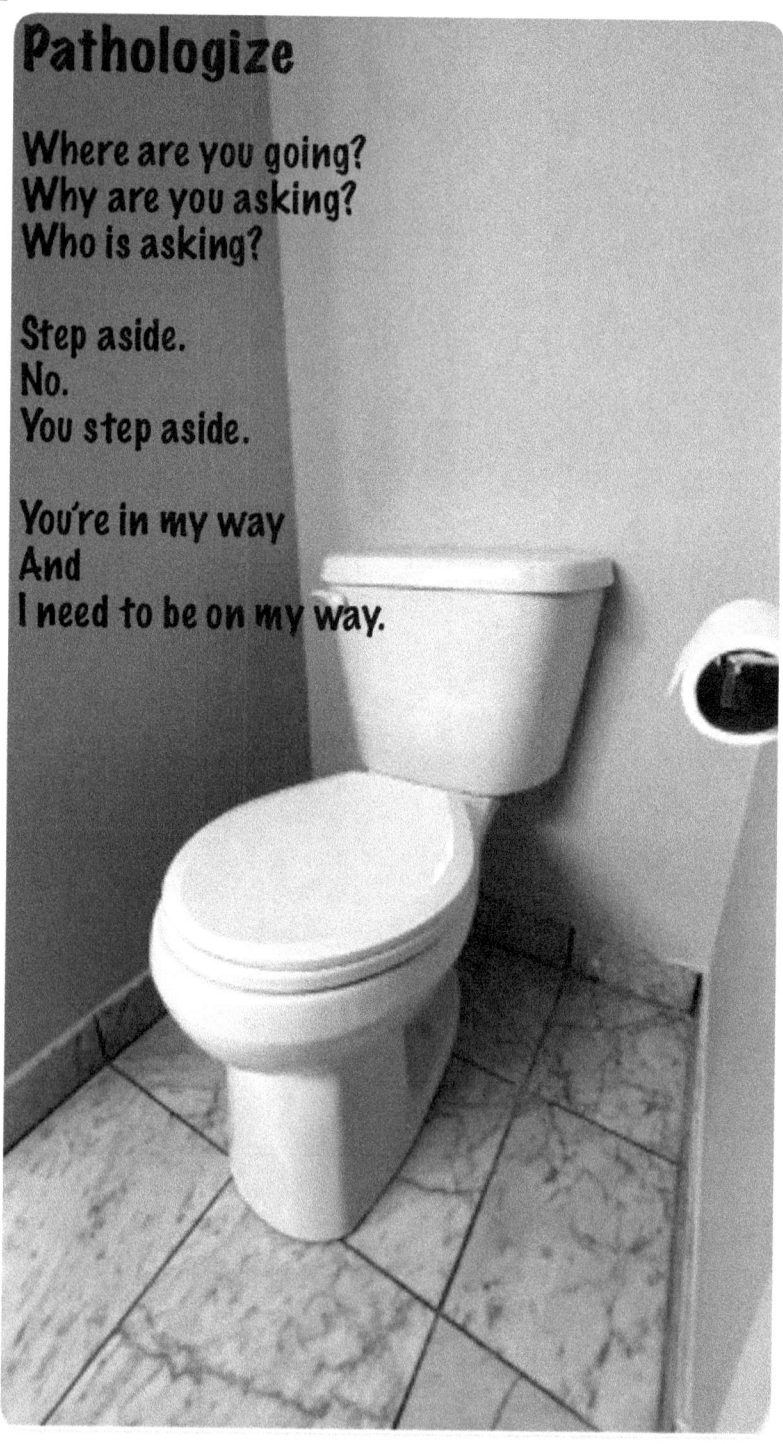

pathologize

Where are you going?
Why are you asking?
Who is asking?

Step aside.
No.
You step aside.

You're in my way
And
I need to be on my way.

Breathe

breathe

<u>thinking</u>

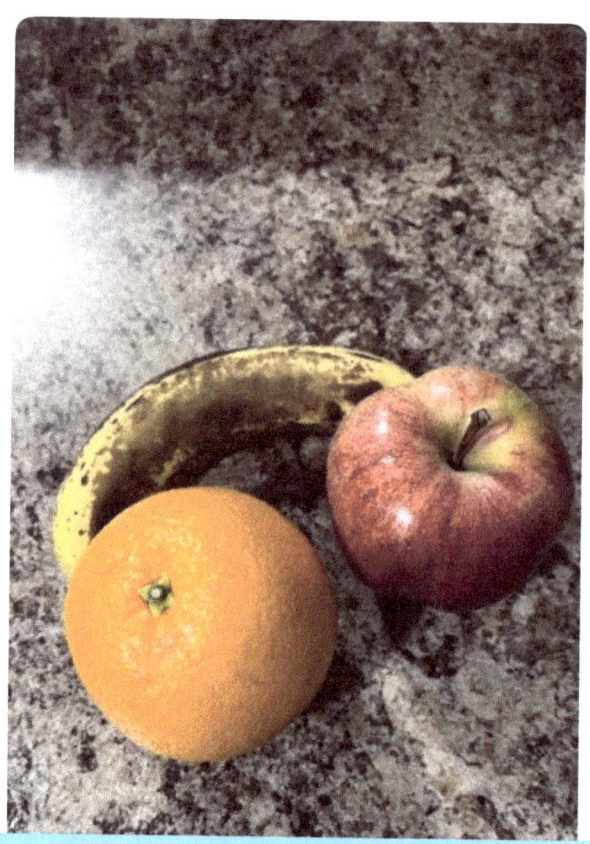

Doing the best I can with what I have and know. My inner voice has served me throughout my life journey. My whole being is a neighborhood. I am a neighbour of my inner voice. We are constantly working out our relationship. It's been a mostly pleasant experience for me. This may not be so for everyone.

It all starts in the mind. If I can nurture my mind towards what's good, admirable, and beneficial, perhaps that's sufficient contribution to my community. "Treat others as you would like to be treated" doesn't always work. Some of us don't treat ourselves quite well. I personally put myself through certain things and demand certain standards from myself that I shouldn't project unto others or expect of them.

Prov. 23:7 NKJV

...inking

...oing the best I can with what I have and know. My inner voice has served ...e throughout my life journey. My whole being is a neighborhood. I am a ...eighbour of my inner voice. We are constantly working out our relationship. ...'s been a mostly pleasant experience for me. This may not be so for ...veryone.

...all starts in the mind. If I can nurture my mind towards what's good, ...dmirable, and beneficial, perhaps that's sufficient contribution to my ...ommunity. "Treat others as you would like to be treated" doesn't always ...ork. Some of us don't treat ourselves quite well. I personally put myself ...hrough certain things and demand certain standards from myself that I ...houldn't project unto others or expect of them.

...rov. 23:7 NKJV

Breathe

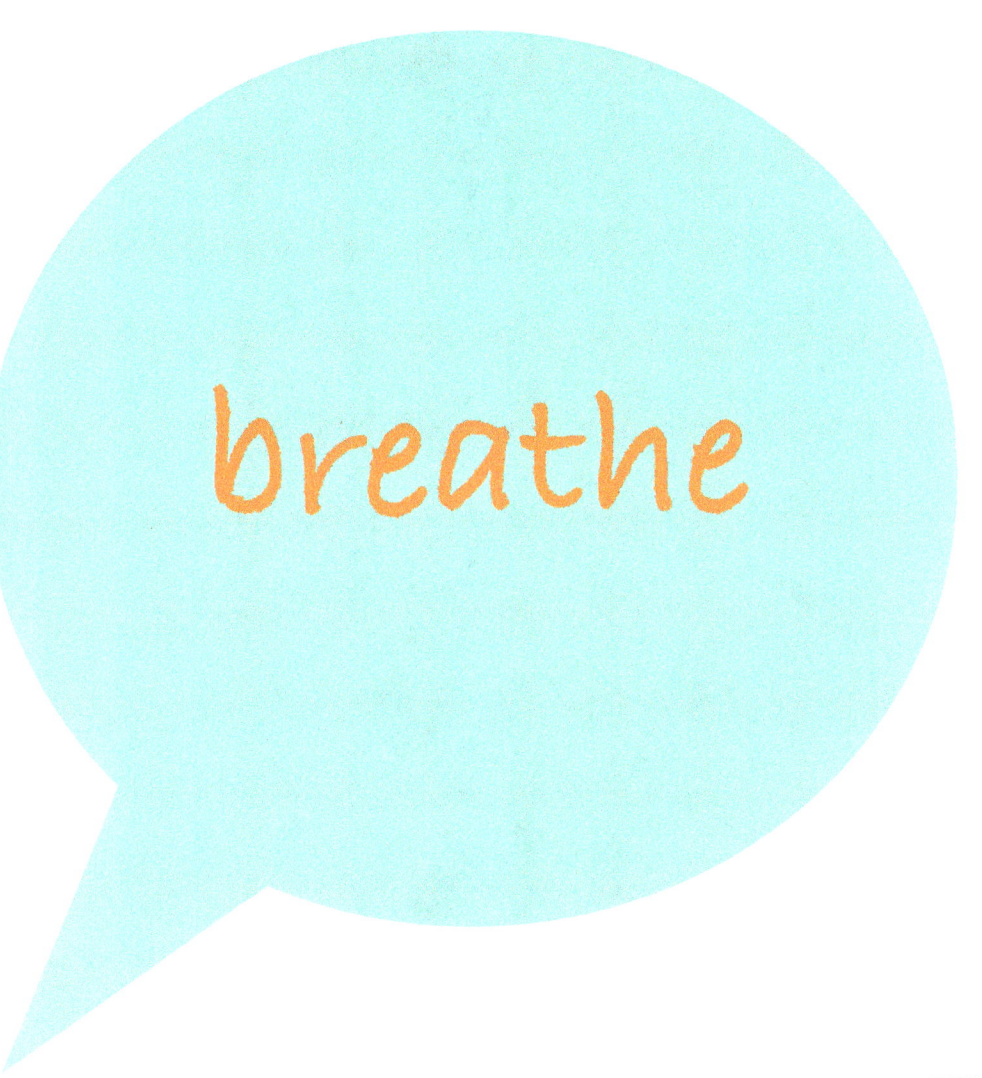

<u>suddenly</u>

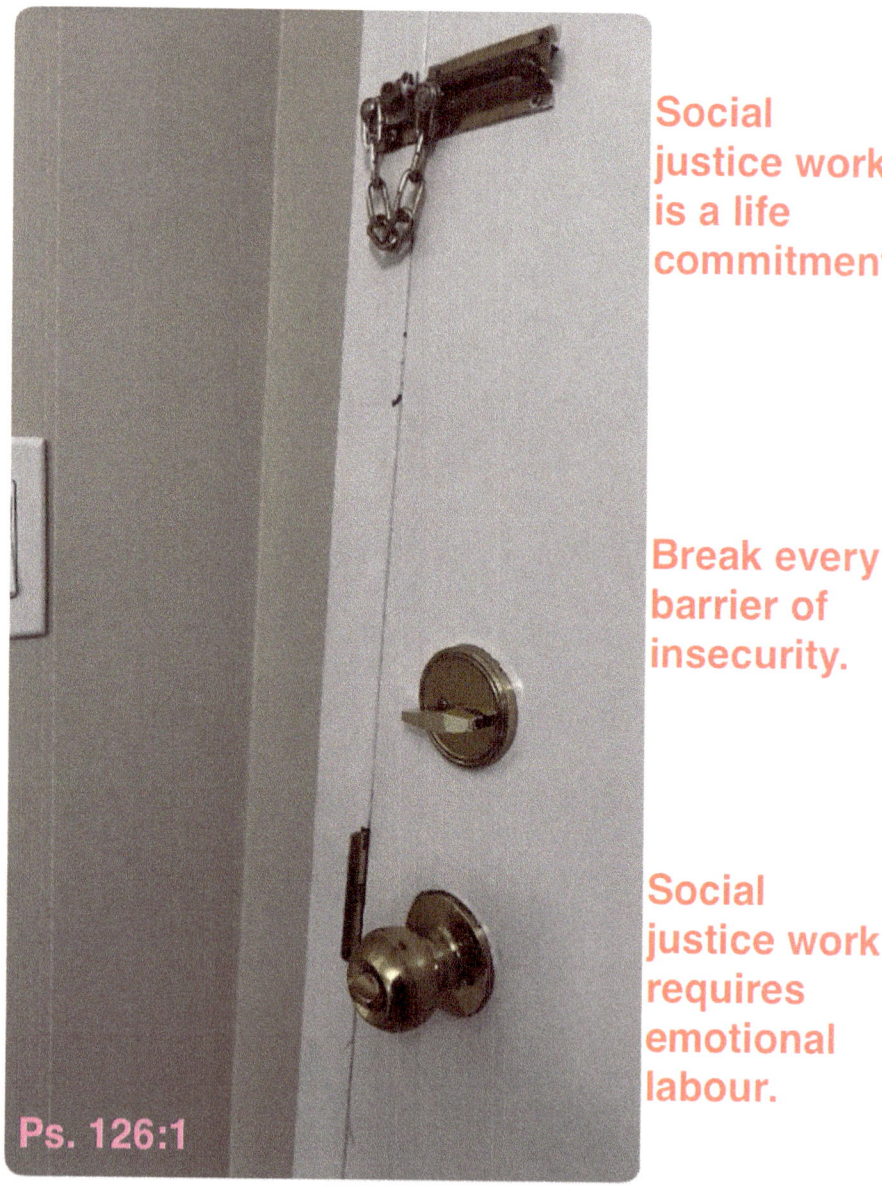

suddenly

Social justice work is a life commitment.

Break every barrier of insecurity.

Social justice work requires emotional labour.

Ps. 126:1

Breathe

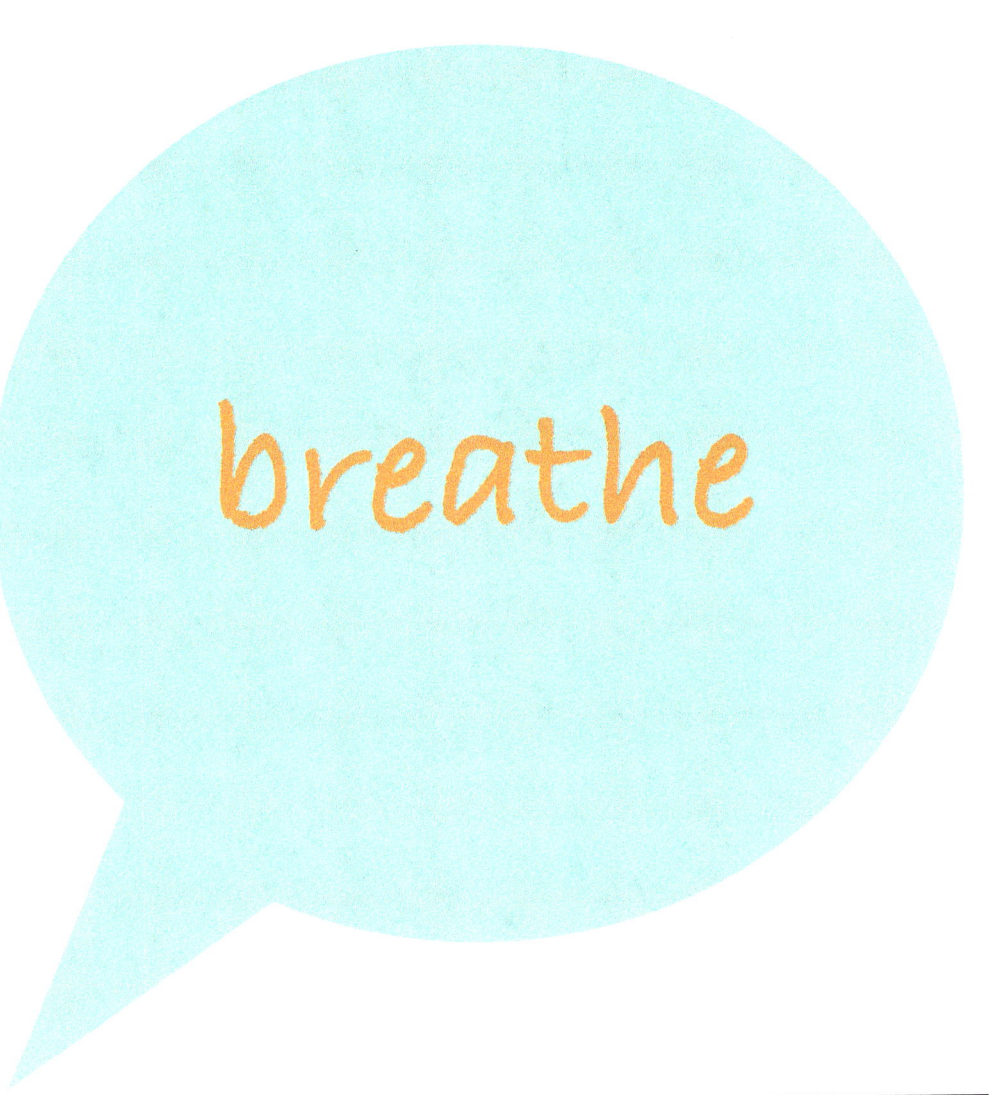

displaced

Sense of displacement. You don't belong in here. This space is only being loaned to you.

Policy. Process. Practice. They're not synonyms. Distinguish between the three.

Clearly articulate the thought process that went into developing your policies and strategies. Outline and document the in-house policies that undergird your external messages. Avoid adopting third party policies and messages that you don't know how and why they were set up.

If you want to develop policies, do the hard work and heavy lifting. If you would rather adopt existing policies, you should at least investigate how and why those policies are in place so you can understand them, be able to explain them to your clients and be able to justify them.

Prepare detailed, documented and well thought out policies, processes and practices for your organization. Your external messaging should be based on thorough and well-documented internal policies that are backed up with tested processes and best practices. Move away from silos and reliance on individual memories.

Develop thorough and documented institutional policies and guidelines. Build quality control mechanisms into your processes and practices. When you choose to adopt or depart from pre-existing policies, practices and messaging, state and justify - to your team internally and in written documented format - why you adopted those policies or took those departures. Build, cultivate and maintain institutional memory. Your successors will thank you for it.

#policy
#strategy
#policywonk
#dreamteam
#silos
#systemic
#institutionalized
#qualitycontrol

Misplaced

...nse of displacement. You don't belong in here. This space is only being loaned to you.

Policy. Process. Practice. They're not synonyms. Distinguish between the three.

Clearly articulate the thought process that went into developing your policies and strategies. Outline and document the in-house policies that undergird your external messages. Avoid adopting third party policies and messages that you don't know how and why they were set up.

If you want to develop policies, do the hard work and heavy lifting. If you would rather adopt existing policies, you should at least investigate how and why those policies are in place so you can understand them, be able to explain them to your clients and be able to justify them.

Prepare detailed, documented and well thought out policies, processes and practices for your organization. Your external messaging should be based on thorough and well-documented internal policies that are backed up with tested processes and best practices. Move away from silos and reliance on individual memories.

Develop thorough and documented institutional policies and guidelines. Build quality control mechanisms into your processes and practices. When you choose to adopt or depart from pre-existing policies, practices and messaging, state and justify - to your team internally and in written documented format - why you adopted those policies or took those departures. Build, cultivate and maintain institutional memory. Your successors will thank you for it.

- policy
- strategy
- policywonk
- dreamteam
- silos
- systemic
- institutionalized
- qualitycontrol

Breathe

breathe

<u>purposeful</u>

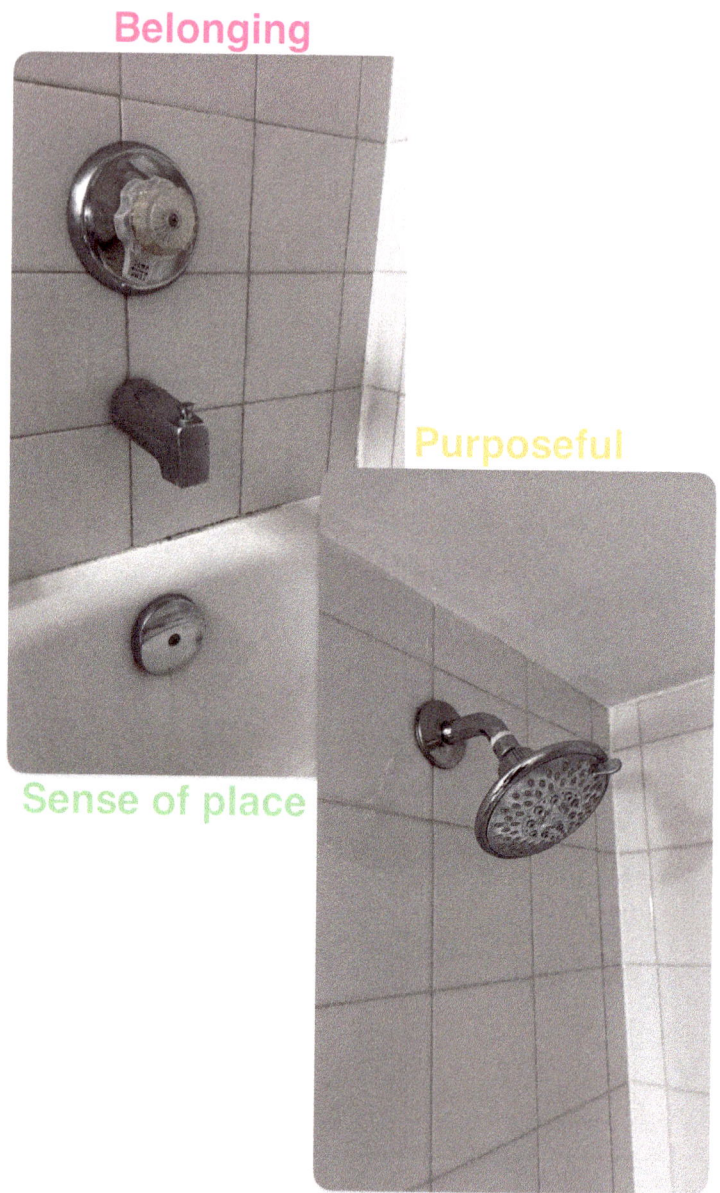

purposeful

Belonging.
Purposeful.
Sense of place.
Orientation.

Breathe

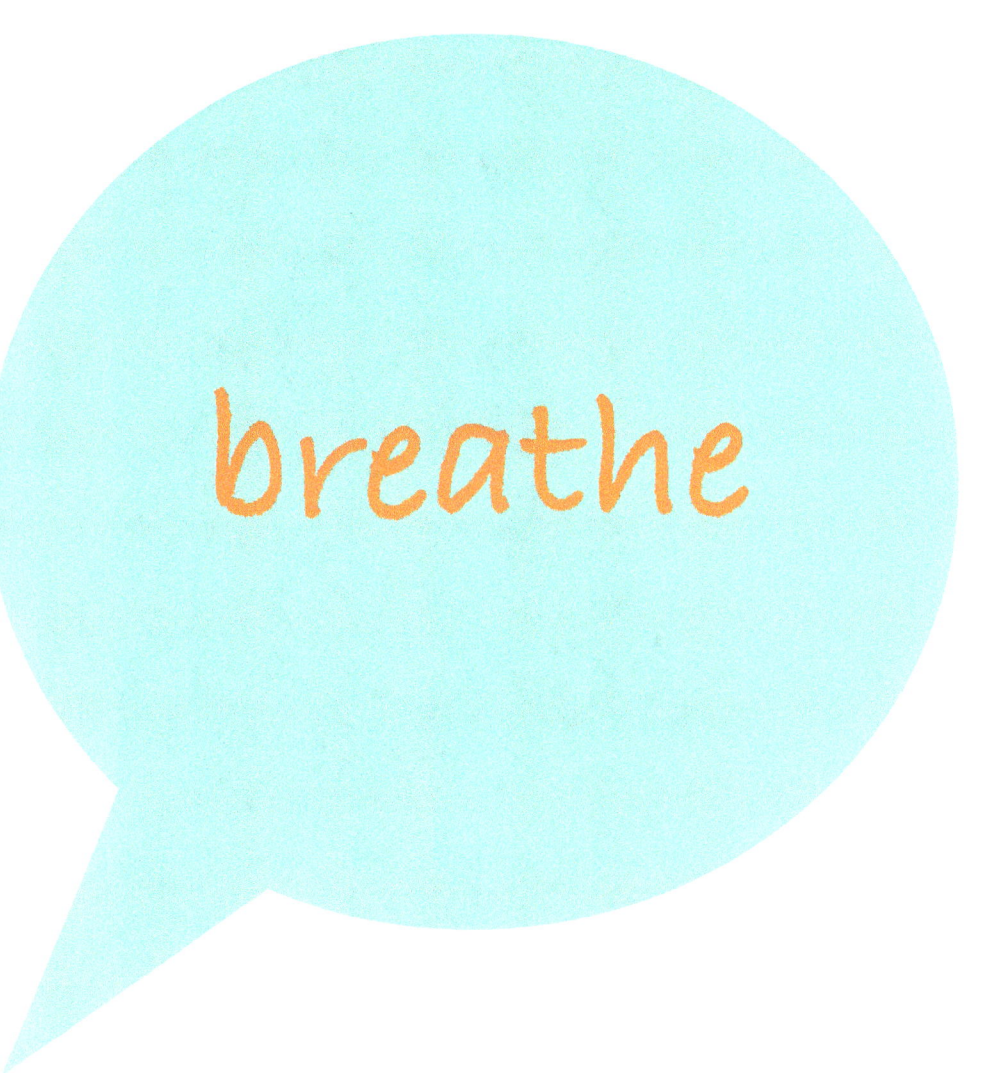

read & write

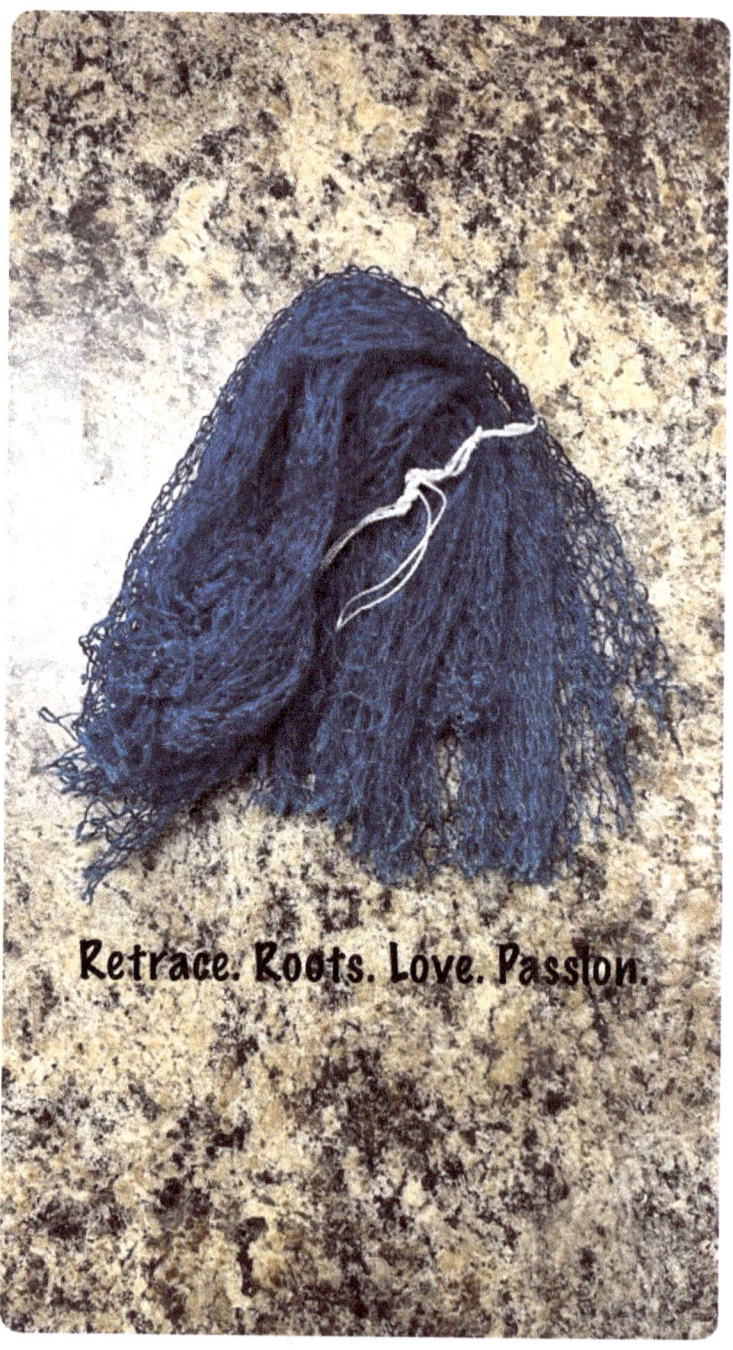

read & write

Retrace.
Roots.
Love.
Passion.

Breathe

breathe

grounded

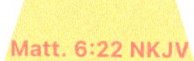
Matt. 6:22 NKJV

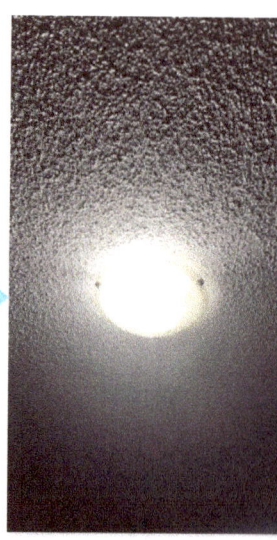

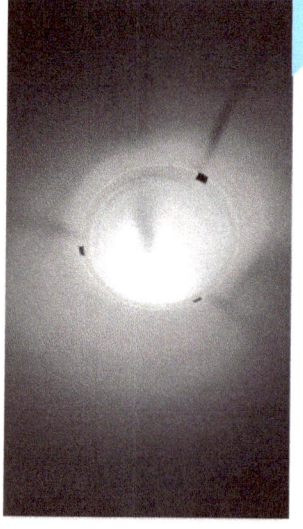

~~Focused. Centred. Grounded.~~

grounded

Focused.
Centred.
Grounded.

Matt. 6:22 NKJV

Breathe

breathe

<u>foot soldier</u>

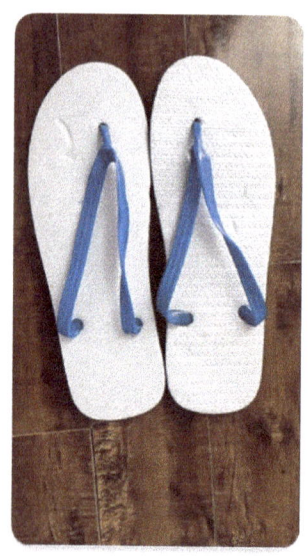

*Foot soldier.
Lord, please help me plant my feet firmly on the ground. I need to be equipped for the emotional labour and heavy lifting.
Being trained for a job doesn't insulate me from injury on the job.*

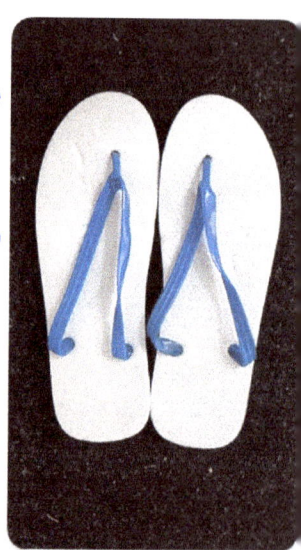

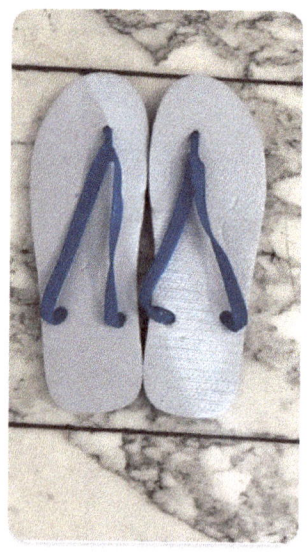

foot soldier

Lord, please help me plant my feet firmly on the ground. I need to be equipped for the emotional labour and heavy lifting. Being trained for a job doesn't insulate me from injury on the job.

Breathe

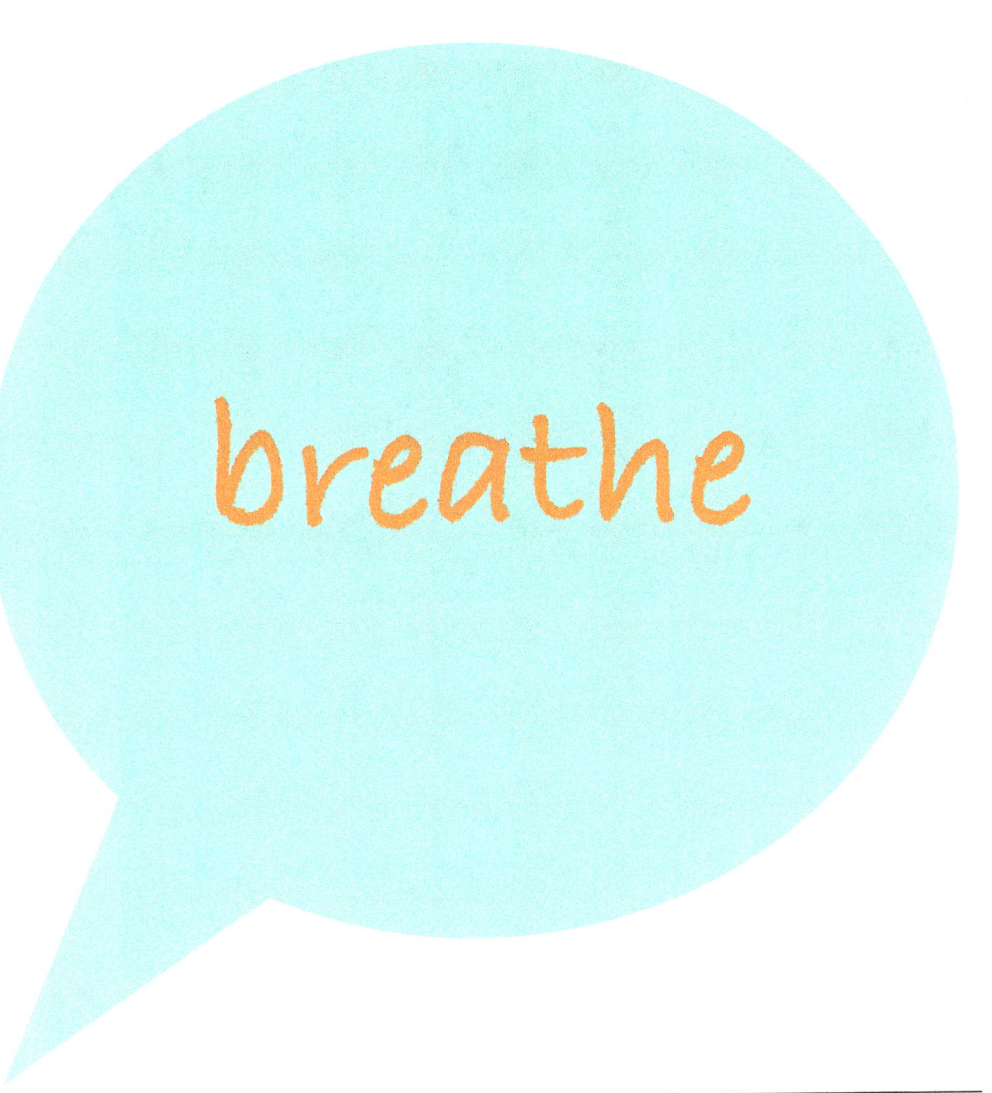

<u>heart</u>

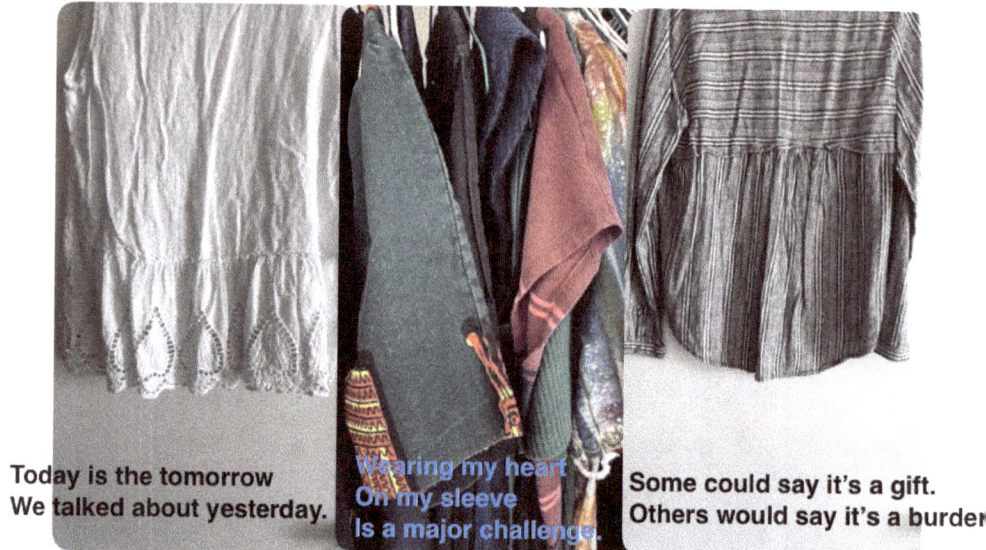

Today is the tomorrow
We talked about yesterday.

Wearing my heart
On my sleeve
Is a major challenge.

Some could say it's a gift.
Others would say it's a burden.

Matt. 12:34 NKJV

heart

Today is the tomorrow
We talked about yesterday.

Wearing my heart
On my sleeve
Is a major challenge.

Some could say it's a gift.
Others would say it's a burden.

Matt. 12:34 NKJV

Breathe

breathe

gaslighting on steroids

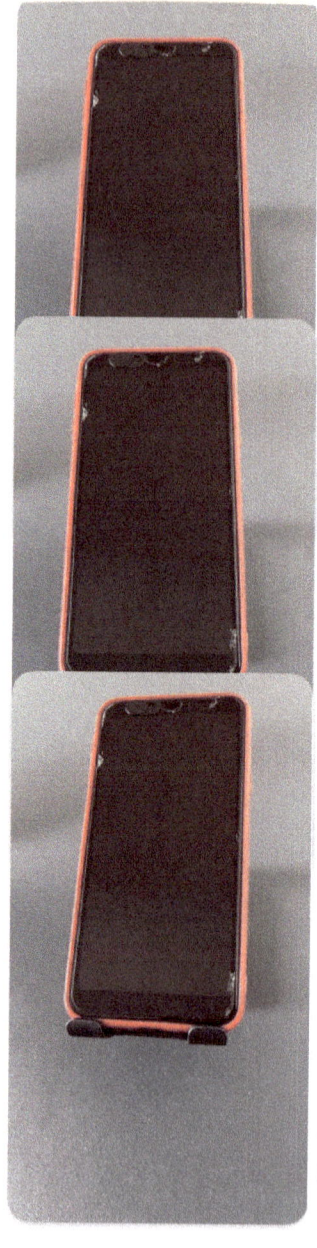

Gaslighting on steroids

People are dealing with issues of paranoia that are potentially triggered by experiences they have with technology. It's gaslighting on steroids. On social media's use of AI, even the intellectual and intelligent ones are confused. Privacy is an illusion. Try figuring out how come a conversation you just had about pain reliever in the privacy of your bedroom – which has deliberately been "unplugged" to give you downtime – brought up multiple pain relief medication adverts when you visit your social media accounts while outside your home the following day. This experience sometimes leaves people perplexed, distressed and disoriented. I've heard conversations between people in which they're asking themselves about these experiences. The algorithm is no respecter of persons. Psychology is playing catch up as it's figuring out some of the effects of AI's and algorithm's manipulative practices on people's perception of reality.

Gaslighting on steroids

People are dealing with issues of paranoia that are potentially triggered by experiences they have with technology. It's gaslighting on steroids. On social media's use of AI, even the intellectual and intelligent ones are confused. Privacy is an illusion. Try figuring out how come a conversation you just had about pain reliever in the privacy of your bedroom – which has deliberately been "unplugged" to give you downtime – brought up multiple pain relief medication adverts when you visit your social media accounts while outside your home the following day. This experience sometimes leaves people perplexed, distressed and disoriented. I've heard conversations between people in which they're asking themselves about these experiences. The algorithm is no respecter of persons. Psychology is playing catch up as it's figuring out some of the effects of AI's and algorithm's manipulative practices on people's perception of reality.

Breathe

breathe

faulty activism

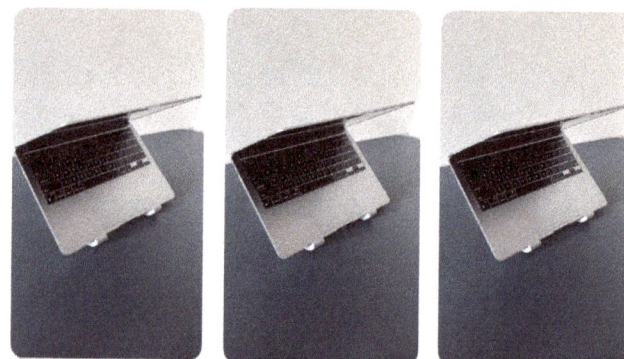

#hashtag activism coupled with couch potatorism and sofa criticism devoid of deep thinking often leads to faulty activism.

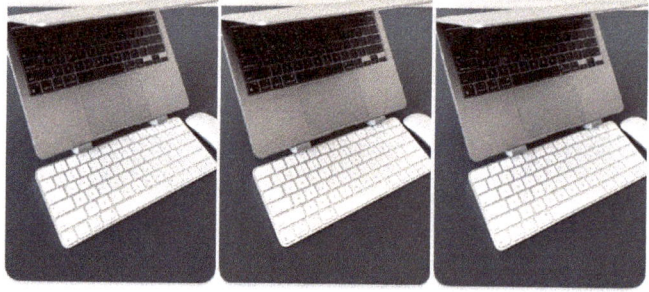

faulty activism

hashtag activism coupled with couch potatorism and sofa criticism devoid of deep thinking often leads to faulty activism.

Breathe

breathe

Acknowledge. Address. Accommodate.

After you have done everything you're able to do, stand

Stand tall.
Stand firm.
Stand bold.
Stand unashamed.
Stand unbended.
Stand vulnerable.
Stand in peace.
Stand in joy.
Stand in love.
Stand in hope.
Stand!

Eph. 6:12-13

Acknowledge. Address. Accommodate.

After you have done everything you're able to do, stand!

Stand tall.
Stand firm.
Stand bold.
Stand unashamed.
Stand unbended.
Stand vulnerable.
Stand in peace.
Stand in joy.
Stand in love.
Stand in hope.
Stand!

Eph. 6:12-13

Breathe

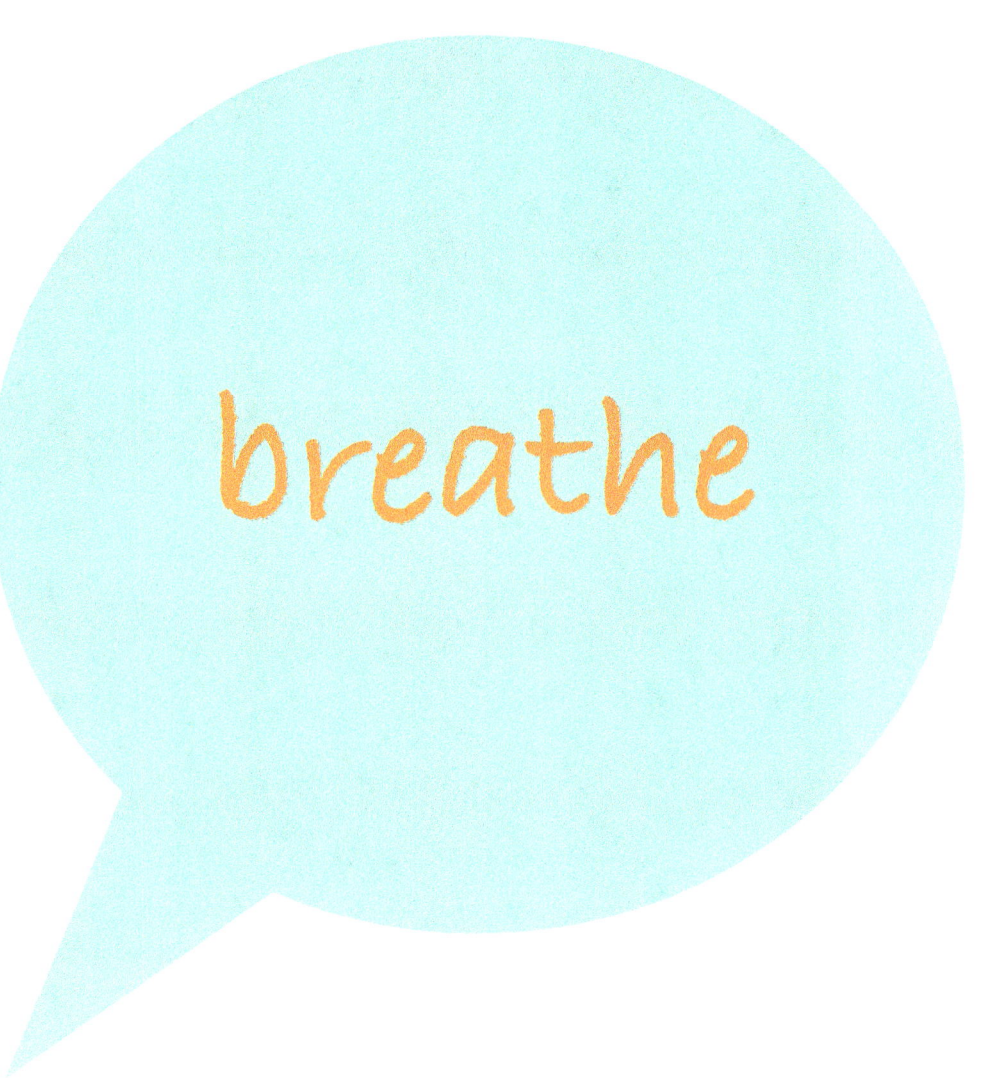

Pregnant silence.

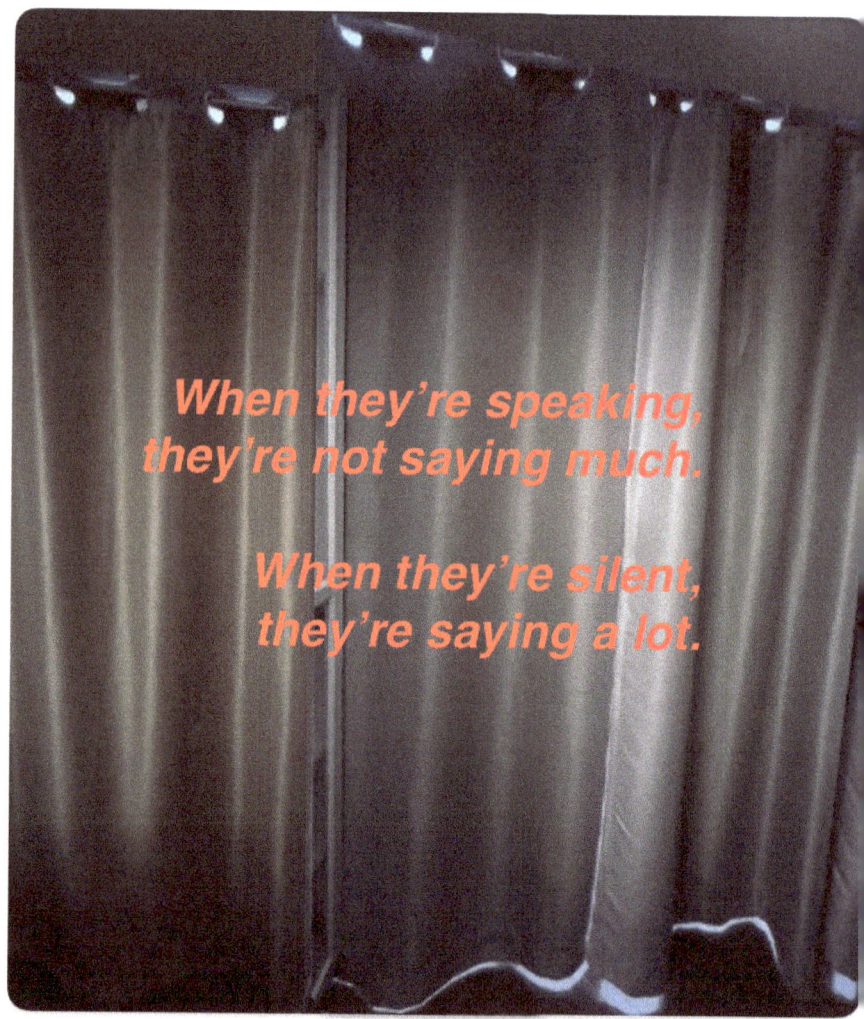

Pregnant silence.

When they're speaking,
they're not saying much.

When they're silent,
they're saying a lot.

Breathe

breathe

Gratitude Attitude

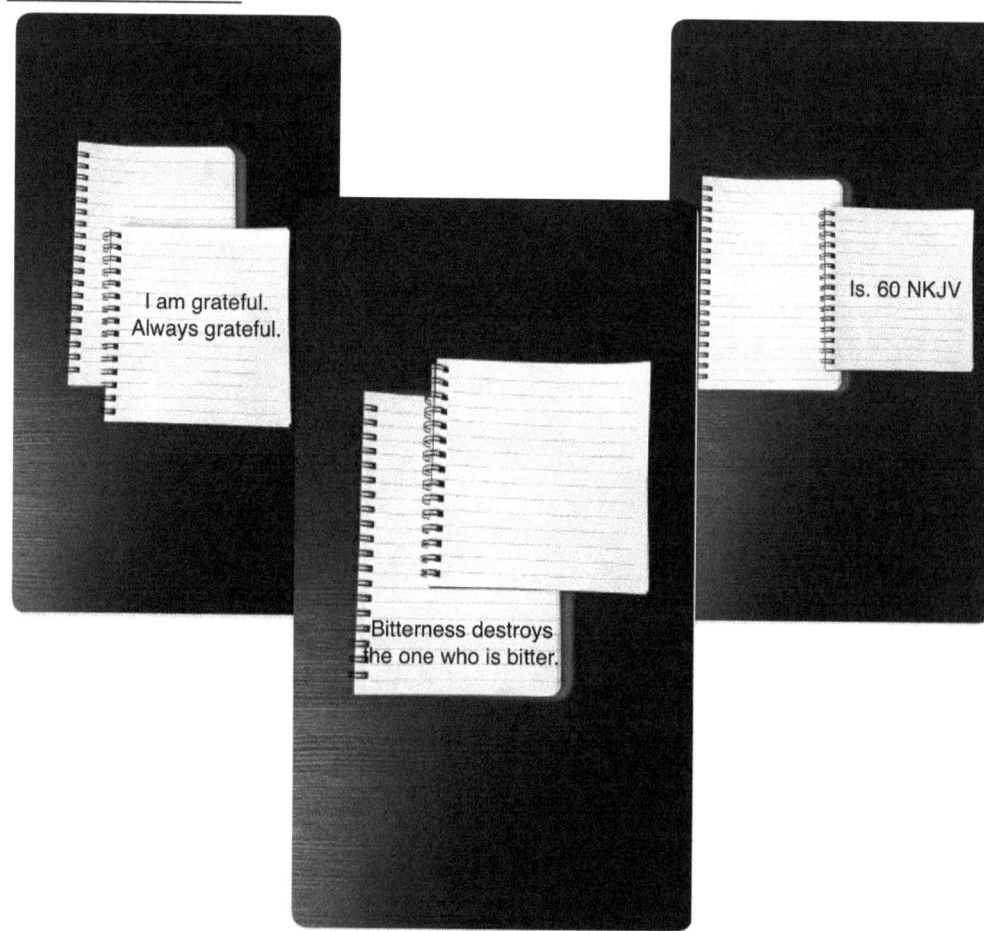

Gratitude Attitude

Bitterness destroys the one who is bitter.

I am grateful.
Always grateful.

Is. 60 NKJV

Breathe

breathe

Got it!

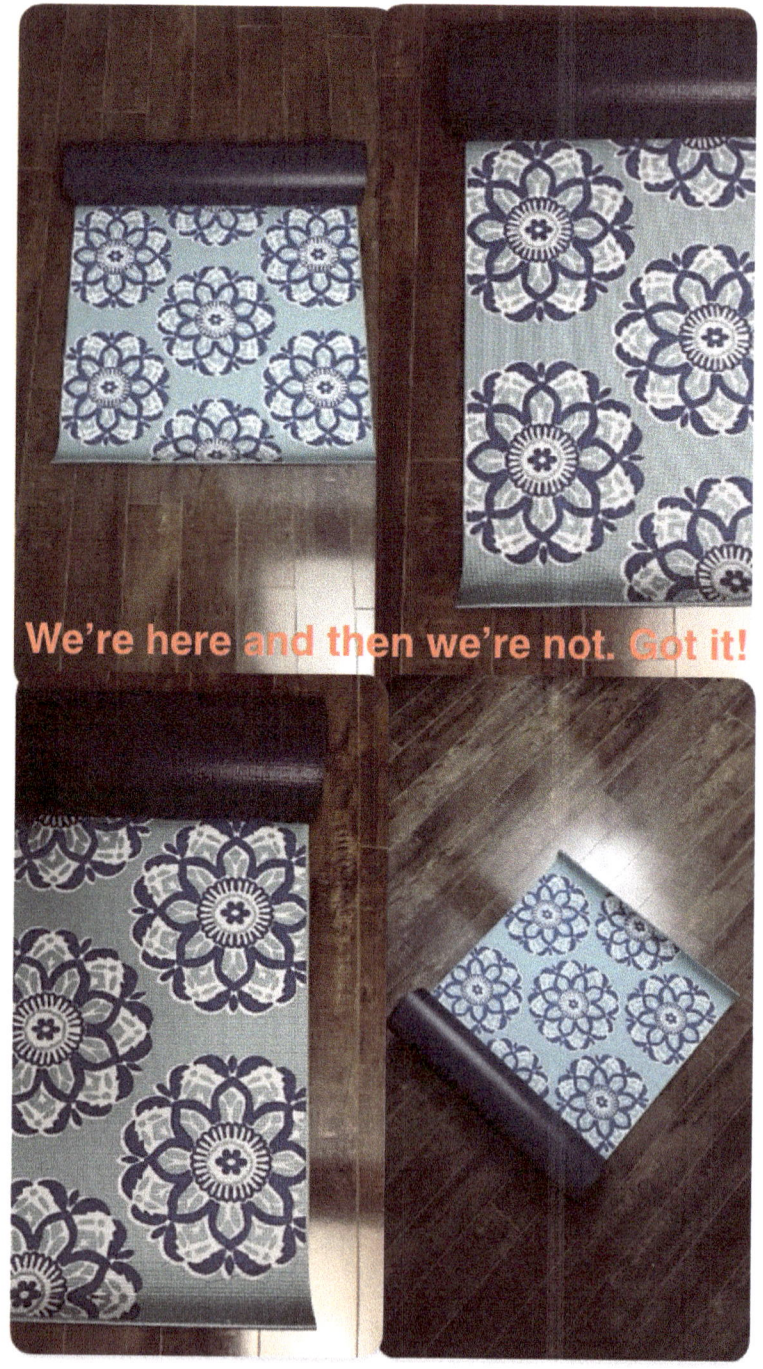

Got it!

We're here and then we're not. Got it!

Breathe

breathe

Rituals

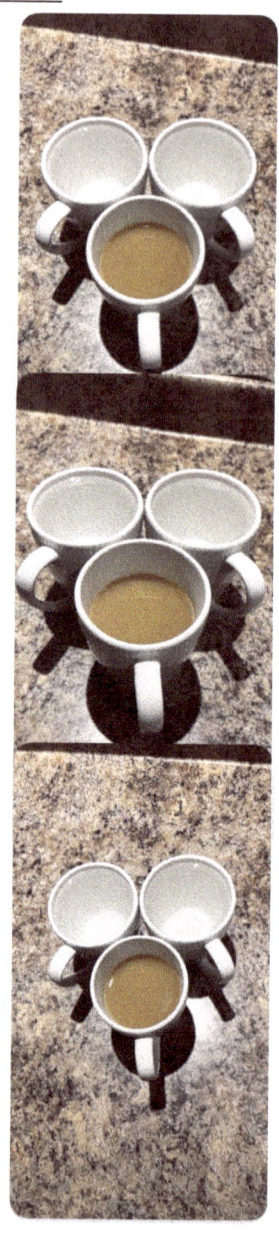

Rituals.

Day in, day out.
It seems darkest at dawn.
Then the day breaks.
You do the morning ritual
It works.
It helps.

Rituals.

Rituals

Day in, day out.
It seems darkest at dawn.
Then the day breaks.
You do the morning ritual.
It works.
It helps.
Rituals.

Breathe

breathe

East looking West

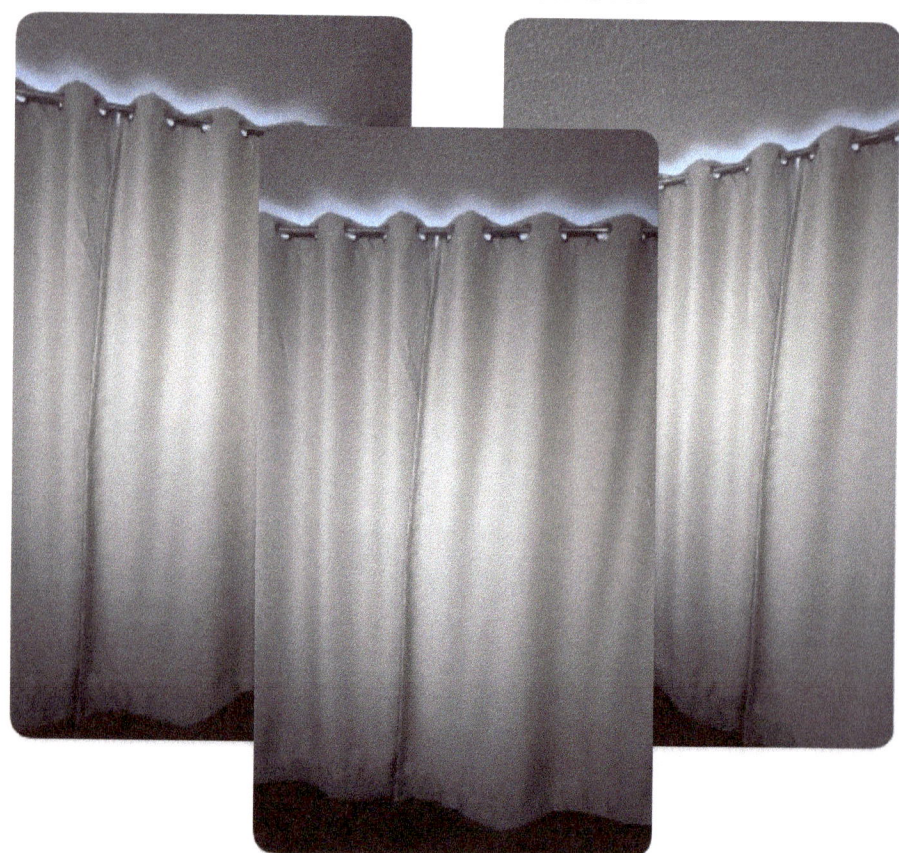

I'm on meditation.

My drug of choice is mindfulness.

East looking West

I'm on meditation.
My drug of choice is mindfulness.

Breathe

breathe

About the author

Jùmọ̀kẹ́ Gíwá is in transit.

Reflecting on spaces, places, and materials that are useful for nurturing and protecting wellness and wealth. Today is the tomorrow we talked about yesterday.

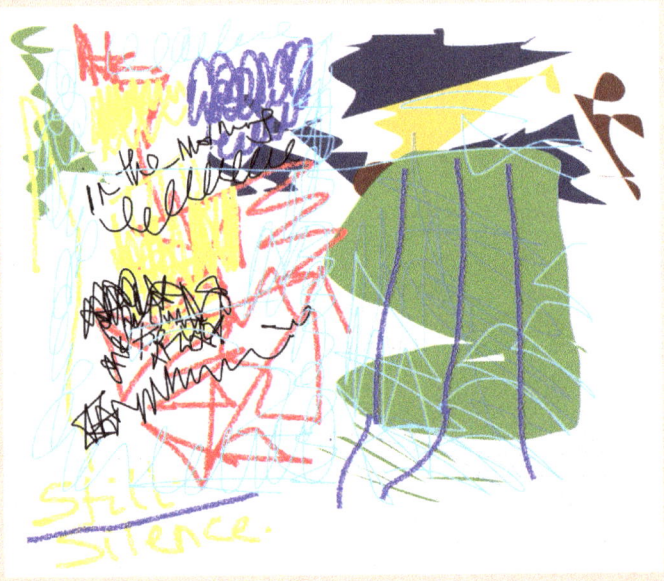

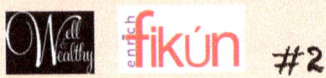

#2